Listen
to Rarely Heard
Voices

Listen to Rarely Heard Voices

by Peter W. Petschauer

MindMend Publishing

OTHER PUBLICATIONS BY THE AUTHOR

Books

Was man so alles lernt; mein Südtiroler Rückhalt für die moderne Welt.
Weger Buchhandlung, 2022

*An Immigrant in the 1960s. Finding Hope and Success
in New York City.* Perspektiven Presse, 2020

Hopes and Fears: Past and Present.
MindMend Publishing, 2019

*A Perfect Portrait,
A Novel about an 18th-Century German Woman Painter.*
Perspektiven Presse, 2016

In the Face of Evil. The Sustenance of Traditions.
Perspektiven Presse, 2014

Der Vater und die SS: Erich Petschauer und das NS-Regime.
Weger Buchhandlung, 2007

Human Space: Finding Our Place in a Threatening World.
Greenwood Press, 1997

*The Language of History:
A Topical Approach to World Civilization.*
Kendall Hunt Pub Co, 1994

*The Education of Women in Eighteenth-Century Germany:
Bending the Ivy.*
Lewiston/Lampeter/Queenston, 1989

Afers, Gedanken zur Geschichte.
Weger Buchhandlung, 1985

A Play

Fellow Traveler
Stage read as part of Appalachian State University's Program of Theatre
and Dance at the Appalachian Summer Festival, 2012.

Other Contributions

Five poems in D. Beisel (Ed.), *Wounded Centuries: A Selection of Poems.*
Circumstantial Productions and Grolier Poetry Press, 2015

More than 300 articles, book chapters und professional presentations.

Dedicated
to my family members and friends
who enabled me
to thrive as a writer and poet

Published in 2022 by the MindMend Publishing Co., NY, NY

Library of Congress Control Number: 2022942863

Cataloging Data:

Petschauer, Peter. Listen to Rarely heard Voices / Peter W. Petschauer

1. Poetry. 2. Psychobiography. 3. Autobiography. 4. Psychohistory. 5. Conscious and unconscious communications. 6. Creativity (literary, artistic, etc.) – Psychological concepts.

ISBN-13: 978-1-942431-20-6 (paperback)

Front Cover Art Credit: Photograph by Peter W. Petschauer, "From an airplane. May 19th, 2019."

Book design, editing, and book cover – by MindMendMedia, Inc. @ MindMendMedia.com

mindmendmedia
piecing it together

TABLE OF CONTENTS

TROUBLES

PUBLISHER'S FOREWORD

"What happens when people open their hearts?"
"They get better." – Haruki Murakami

After publishing *Hopes and Fears: Past and Present* in 2019, we are once again drawn to the engaging poetry of Peter Petschauer, a "consummate weaver of words" (as Dr. Noyes Capehart called the author in his endorsement of the first volume of poetry). Dr. Petschauer, an esteemed international scholar, writes with the wisdom and experience of his life and never misses a beat. His background includes growing up in the mountains of Italy removed from the atrocities of the Nazis and the knowledge of his father's association with the SS. His humble beginnings kept him in hiding and with four different women engaging in the role of his mother. Peter's poems are the ultimate celebration of a life well lived in generosity of spirit and compassion, evidenced by a kindly and helpful disposition towards all around him.

Long a citizen of the U.S. and professor of history, his sharply focused eyes bring new awareness to all he sees as he enlightens our many paths. Interspersed with the poems are wonderful photographs, most taken by the author, illuminating his poems and their environment.

His new book is divided into three sections: Nature, Life, and Troubles. His oneness and joy of nature is constantly apparent. In one of the book's earliest poems, "FALL WALK," he writes:

"Birds complain about my presence,
acorns crash to the ground,
leaves jump to the side,
rustle as they reach the border of the path…"

Or in "THE CARPETED PATH":

"Along the path nature does the talking,
we embrace its call."

In the "LIFE" section, Peter Petschauer brilliantly combines the pain and positives of aging, as in his poem "EVOLUTION'S EVOLUTION": "(t)he pain of aging brings serenity and wisdom," and in his reminiscing poem "OTHER TIMES":

"Tentacles of other times
reaching into the present.
The illusion of being young forever"

And from "LIFE SOUNDS," the quietly joyful:

"The soft breathing of my beloved partner
in a shared bed.
Reassurances of life"

Every poem brings its subjects to life at their reading, easily painting pictures for our minds to participate in Peter's world. In the section "TROUBLES," the author brilliantly renders the politically troubled times we now inhabit and the miscalculations dominating our lives. In "ALL POWERFUL EMPIRES," he writes:

"Are we learning from this accumulation of lessons?
History offers this resounding answer:
You have the singular capacity
to ignore the lessons of the past."

In Peter's poem "CREATING IMAGES," one feels an update to the children's folk tale "THE EMPEROR'S NEW CLOTHES" illustrated repeatedly. And in his "THE RETURN OF THE AUTHORITARIANS," "Once more pretty slogans cover the evil underneath/ Reactivating glorious pasts that rarely were," Petschauer's poems, particularly in this section, urge applause.

On behalf of our publishing team, the international psychohistorical community at large, and all who are engaged with life "here and now" – I am thankful to Peter for his dedication to humanity and nature, to history and psychohistory, for his empathic stance in many difficult situations, and his courage and vulnerability, which are so rare in today's world!

Peter's poetry opens our hearts, and we all "get better"!

Inna Rozentsvit,

MindMend Publishing,
Editor-in-Chief

ACKNOWLEDGEMENTS

As always with complicated writing projects, many individuals are involved in completing the task. Dr. David Beisel, university professor, author, and friend was the first to encourage me to write poetry and to share it with others. It is hard to imagine that we have known each other since graduate school at New York University. David published five of my earliest poems in his book, *Wounded Centuries. A Selection of Poems* (David Beisel, Ed., Grolier Poetry Press and Circumstantial Productions, 2016, pp. 47-53). Without his encouragement during a ride and conversation in his car from his home to one of his classes in 2015, I would not have thought it feasible to explore poetry as my primary writing form. A splendid gift. Thank you very much, David.

Dr. Howard Stein's poetry appeals to me more than almost any other contemporary approach. Howard and I discovered each other years ago over bagels in NYC; since then, the friendship has flourished in spite of being separated by thousands of miles and our very different backgrounds. He has read practically every one of the poems in this book, and the one before it, and offered meaningful suggestions to each. If Basho inspired me to write short and succinct poems, Howard ensured that each was in passable English and made its point well. Thank you, Howard, for being there always.

Dr. Zohara Boyd, my friend and colleague, encouraged me many times as we rode to and from talks at schools and colleges to speak about our separate experiences during WWII and the Holocaust. Her family hid in Warsaw in plain sight in the early 1940s and I grew up on a farm in the mountains of Italy's South Tyrol. Her father understood the Gestapo's plans and he decided, brilliantly I must add, to take his wife, her younger sister and infant Zohara into the Polish capital and not a nearby forest where they would surely have been detected. I grew up on the Egarter farm in Afers above Brixen/Bressanone because the owner persuaded my father and mother to let my brother and me stay in her care to avoid the war. "You have got to write about this," I hear her say to this day. Thank you with all my heart, Zo.

Dr. Paul Elovitz, also a university professor, author, and friend has played a unique role in this phase of my life. He is the editor of *Clio's Psyche* and asked me many years ago to be on the editorial board of this refereed journal. He too has read most of my poems, but he also read all of my essays, whether they were published in *Clio* or in another journal. Paul is one of those men who may hesitate to say what needs to be corrected in an essay, poem, or even a book, but he will say it and that is what makes the friendship we have built so important – his forthrightness and honesty. Thank you too, Paul.

Writing, creativity, takes place best in a household in which one partner supports the other in their quest. My wife Joni creates a home in which writing can take place daily, even if some days it's only a paragraph or two or the first draft of a poem; other days it will be hourlong sessions behind the computer. Those who write this way know that during these short or long sessions emerges page upon page in a relatively short time. The joy is in the writing itself and in the realization that it is supported and appreciated. Thank you, Joni, my love.

Some authors create without the support, moral and otherwise, of family, friends, and colleagues. I am one who cannot. This is why this volume is dedicated to them. The family and friends in the US and in Germany, Austria, and Italy. Thanks to the Internet, most of us can be in touch regularly and thus can be "closer" to each other than in the so-called "good old days" and more readily share our thoughts and activities. I thank all of you for your friendship and support; *danke Euch herzlich für Eure Freundschaft und Unterstützung.*

This is my second poetry book that Inna Rozentsvit has edited and published through MindMend Publishing, Inc. Dr. Rozentsvit is an extraordinary human being. An immigrant like me, but at a much more difficult time for immigrants than I experienced earlier in the US, she has written beautifully about her family's difficult past in Ukraine and her struggles with it. In spite of obstacles, she persevered and is now a major voice and truly engaged scholar and leader and of our small group of psychohistorians. We would be lost without her administrative and technical skills. Inna publishes thoughtfully edited books for diverse authors; her enthusiasm for the published word, whatever its form, seems to have no limits. Thank you.

Most books I have published have enjoyed the experienced and astute hand of Judy Geary's editing. What a gift and profound staying power to read, correct, and cajole, and then read and correct again in the hope that the author will heed her advice. I do because "I know better." Ms. Geary has never failed in word or deed. Judy, I am most grateful to you for subtle insights and the many corrections you have given my work.

FROM THE AUTHOR: ON A PERSONAL NOTE

We hardly ever know when or where we made the turn that took us into our later life and its possibilities and challenges.

I became intrigued with language as early as seven or eight. My teacher in a village *Volksschule* (elementary school) in the mountains of Northern Italy taught me to write German script. The stylized form appealed to me, and I have used my knowledge of it several times to interpret or translate documents written in script. This includes translating the notes of a couple who escaped Krakow, thinking they could survive in Warsaw. Erna Karpf died during the summer of 1940, and Joseph Karpf – most likely during the winter of 1941, a year after the ghetto had been established.

Initially I did not appreciate having to tackle Latin and Greek, but Caesar's *Gallic War*, Homer's *Odyssey*, and Xenophon's *Anabasis*, in their original language, brought them to life. Reading and memorizing Homeric verses at first seemed an imposition, but they gained a lasting foothold. Much later, the male centeredness of that world became a major topic in my Women's History courses.

Writing in English, after I came to the US in 1957, at the outset was again a chore, but with time I realized how much smoother English flowed than German and began to enjoy expressing myself in it. Never mind that English is still close to the middle-high German dialect I spoke as a child in the village. Once I discovered the study of history, and the almost forgotten advice of Leopold von Ranke that one must endeavor to discover the past as it was, writing it became such a joy that I published articles and books, one after the other.

Once I found the Japanese poet Matsuo Basho during the World Civilization courses, a new possibility of writing opened up. If history writing is observing the past and debating with others, in complex formulations, about this or that topic, poetry allows me to observe in the immediate and without the voices of others proposing directions for me to take, be it traditional history or psychohistorical writing. In poetry I can represent my voice succinctly. I can tackle a historical topic or the beauty of bees following their purpose in springtime, or highlight the abuses of dictators and autocrats, or the not so subtle reflections about a pile of horse apples.

As a historian and sometime psychohistorian, I lean toward historical topics. That in turn may lead to a more traditional approach to poetry. It fits better with the Homeric epics and the works of Goethe and Schiller I read as a child and young adult. Then too, of the great poets whom I read occasionally to seek inspiration about approach and style, the Japanese poet Basho is my favorite. Every so often I endeavor to compose in his brilliantly succinct style. Exactitude in observing and meaning. To be sure, I do not compare myself to the masters.

Some underwent a difficult childhood; some others enjoyed a supportive one. Some suffered traumatic events that intruded on them in early life; others floated through without a scratch.

Some enjoy their pessimism. Others work with what is given. Some prefer a more traditional approach to poetry; others almost tell a story without the traditional line breaks.

In my case, I had a supportive childhood; it helped to deal later with the trauma of discovering my father's association with the SS; working it out became the task of a lifetime. As a consequence, my fear of authoritarians and others who set out to undermine democracies.

Family plays a larger role as well this time. Losing two family members in Italy during a single month in 2020 was a shock that continues to reverberate. I recognized that I am getting older, with family members drifting into dementia. That is why I tackled that difficult transition in some of the poems.

Because my wife and I live in a lovely town near a small lake in the mountains of NC, several poems are about the seasons there and the path to the lake. The path and the lake give us time to contemplate and appreciate our good fortune. Because we live in Europe every year for extended periods of time, many poems are set in Bavaria where we have rented the same apartment since fall of 2010. There I write most about nature and am generally in a happier mode.

Sometimes I write the opposite of the expected. With Bill Dunlap's winter scene, I did not place myself and the reader in it, but rather enjoyed the pleasure of curling up under it by our fire.

Of course, there had to be something about music, books and art ... the focus of my life before and since my retirement in 2006.

INTRODUCTION

Come and cherish these poems about us, human beings, and nature –
from love to hate,
understanding and confusion,
inconvenience and terror.

These human conditions have been elucidated often before; I know.
Still, here is another attempt to have them make sense.

These poems are personal, like most poetry,
but the conditions described are ordinary and familiar.

With my imagery,
I hope to highlight our commonality
and surprise with uniqueness.

NATURE

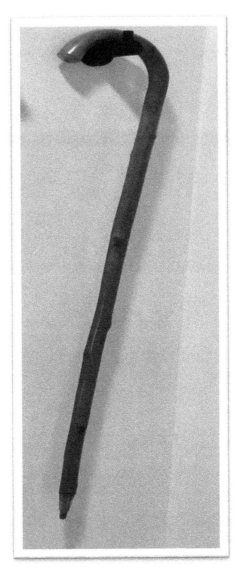

Great-Grandfather's walking stick. Photograph by
Peter W. Petschauer, July 11th, 2021.
Stick and photograph are in the author's inventory.

GREAT-GRANDFATHER'S WALKING STICK
(2018)
For Robert (Bob) Webb

It is no more than a bent piece of bamboo
decades older than I.
The iron tip still affixed with a tiny nail,
not rusted even now.
Just the right height,
as if made for me.

It was my grandfather's,
my mother said long ago.
Max Dalmer, MD,
my great-grandfather,
served as a doctor in WWI.
No bullet touched him then,
no need to serve in WWII.
Practiced in Bernburg,
led the hospital there.
Discovered staph infections of the ear,
wrote about them in 1906.

The truck driver drove through a red light.
He did not see it,
nor the old man,
who perished at nearly 92.

I see him in photographs:
Comfortable in full dress uniform
in a studio-chair,
sitting proudly before his three sons,
they too in their Prussian attire.
In the hiatus between the wars
at the North Sea's Langeoog,
on his daily constitutional,
fully dressed in coat and tie,
bent to his right –
his walking stick hidden behind his back.
Resting from a game of *tamburello*,
his two admiring granddaughters.

Before back surgeries became routine,
staffs supported bodies in decline.
Dr. Dalmer walked daily,
his cane over his right shoulder.
Thus the obituary read in 1942.

Perfect supports,
unceremoniously called sticks today.

Originally published in
Petschauer, P. (2020). *An Immigrant in the 1960s. Finding Hope and Success in New York City.* Perspektiven Presse. (pp. 30-31)

Photograph of Margarethe Stute's painting (c. 1910)*
by Peter W. Petschauer, August 21st, 2021.
Painting and photograph are in author's inventory.

**THREE MOMENTS –
VENETIAN PERSPECTIVES AROUND 1900
(2021)**

It hung in my study since my mother's death –
grandmother Margarethe Stute's Venetian scene.
A strikingly similar creation was mounted in the dining room
of a well-to-do collector –
now serving the same culinary purpose in *The Inn of Brevard* –
Benevenuto Nicholas, the creator of this splendid piece.
The instant of recognition came on July 31st, 2021,

in this very same dining room –
as I feasted on a sumptuous meal in the company of friends –
dishes fit for that other time.

Benevenuto Nicholas created this work before his death in
1900. Original painting is shown in the dining room of the
Inn of Brevard, Brevard, NC.
Photograph by Peter W. Petschauer, July 31st, 2021.
Photograph is in the author's inventory.

Joni, my wife, spotted Nicholas' Venetian scene –
so similar to grandmother's work with its perfect location,
the hues so vibrant and so Venetian –
the same oarsmen plying their trade.

With the harbor to the right,
Nicholas' well-preserved oil places a row of houses on the left –
just as grandmother did in hers,
and the campanile of St. Marco's in the distance.
Unlike his –
houses enclose her "street scene" on both sides.
One oarsman struggles in the foreground with an oar,
another guides his gondola with two festive passengers.
Not tourists to be sure –
they wear Venetian attire.

Postcard from the 19th-century. Taken from the Internet.

But then questions arose about the postcard
that surely originated at the same spot –
most likely at the same time.
Did the Venetian artist create this card for sale?
Did she buy one?
Like a pencil of a Genovese street hanging on one of our walls.
Or did she simply copy him?
Did they use a similar postcard as their source?
Or better still:
Did they take photographs of the scene
                        and paint from it in their studios?

Multilayered questions remain unanswered –
yet we can be certain:
One hung once in the living room of a streetcar engineer
on the lower Rhine,
the other – hangs on the wall in the dining room
of an avid collector in the mountains of North Carolina.

*Margarethe, great-grandfather's daughter-in-law, my grandmother on mother's side, created this oil painting either during or after the honeymoon with my grandfather Kurt in the spring of 1910. They visited at least Venice and Genoa, from where we have a small pen drawing dated 1910.

Photograph by Peter W. Petschauer, Spring 2021.
Photograph is in the author's inventory.

CONVERGENCE
(2021)

Walking deep in thought on the path to the lake,
our steps muffled by a bed of leaves.
Sunshine filtered through the trees,
a slight breeze added to our comfort.
A crow welcomed our arrival in her territory,
or
did she warn her comrades of two large figures?
A lone bird pecked in nearby dirt and
no other hikers were in sight.

They moved toward us,
as if out of the thin air,
a woman and a man –
ahead of them, a stroller.

We pulled masks over mouth and nose –
they wore none.
Behind them just as suddenly a female runner.
She pulled her mask up as well,
when she spotted the four of us.

Five adults and a sleeping baby
converged in a slight bend of an empty path,
as if part of a deliberately orchestrated arrangement.

We separated as quickly as we had met.
The comforting sounds of the waterfall filled the air
as we continued on our way.

On our return to the spot –
parents and baby stood as if fixed to this place,
a bow now on the girl's few strands of hair.

Awakened from her nap –
she voiced her discomfort to the stillness,
father and mother alternating to find relief for her distress.

We replaced our masks,
they remained without –
it seemed they had enough to do without adding one more task.

We were after all ten feet apart
and no other walkers strode the path.

The silence remained disturbed by this other voice.

Photograph by Peter W. Petschauer, October 18th, 2020.
Photograph is in the author's inventory.*

FALL WALK
(2020-2021)

Walking this fall morning,
footsteps part of many noises.

Birds complain about my presence,
acorns crash to the ground,
leaves jump to the side,
rustle as they reach the border of the path.

Nature speaking.

*I took the photograph on the side of the path that leads to Bass Lake
in Blowing Rock, NC.

One of the author's favorite fall photos of Bass Lake, Blowing Rock, NC. Photograph by Peter W. Petschauer, Fall 2018. Photograph is in the author's inventory.

FALL AT THE LAKE
(2018)

The sun's glass-clear rays
spread their golden hue over our valley.
Except for pine and rhododendron,
trees stand bare and ashen.
The undergrowth looks tan,
falling leaves quietly overcome radiant green.
Cool winds play noisy tunes in treetops –
the lake's overflow noisily washes rocks.

While their shoes crush hardening leaves –
walkers' silhouettes turn to shadows.

A tail-twitching squirrel warns of its presence.
Tiny birds chirp an evening's final message.
In the distance, a dog barks at the unknown.

Floating on the water's film,
dampening leaves resist the pull from below.
Fall has arrived at the lake.

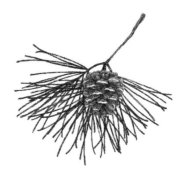

THE CARPETED PATH*
(2020)

It looks and feels like a carpet –
the fallen leaves cover our path.
They color it brown and yellow,
here and there in green and red.
Pine needles make a perfect bed for each of them.
Others cling adamantly to their branches,
not yet ready to begin their descent and
to face the end of their season on the ground.

The sun has chased away the fog –
here and there its golden rays guide our steps.
A strong wind rushes through the remaining leaves
                                        high up in the oaks.
Memories of ocean waves playing along the shore.
Down here on the path
a gentle breeze disturbs a few leaves.

We are alone,
no crow announces our presence.
Most tourists have left and
the locals are lingering over a cup of coffee –
their computer screens can wait a bit longer.
Working from home does have its benefits.

Our feet stir up some leaves.
We recollect our childhoods, when we played
                                in piles of them "at home."
We hear a parent's voice, "Get out of there ...
                                I just finished raking."
The playful voice still rings in our ears –
we did not heed its intent.

Along the path nature does the talking,
we embrace its call.

*The carpet is created by millions of needles that the huge Ponderosa
pines shed during spring; the trees line the path to Bass Lake, Blowing
Rock, NC.

A fresh pile of horse apples.
Photograph by Peter W. Petschauer, June 17th, 2021.
Photograph is in the author's inventory.

HORSE APPLES
(2015-2021)

Horse apples along the path,
steam still rising,
fresh and odiferous,
clearly formed and smooth,
dark brown interwoven with undigested stems.

Deposited minutes ago –
a unique reminder of horses' permissiveness.

A deposit such as this,
at another time,
in another place.
A find to be cherished,
not to be admired by the poet.
Two sisters in search of fuel –
looked about to see if anyone was watching,
bent down,
and scooped up their auspicious haul
in Württemberg after WWII.

Forests had yielded no more twigs –
and other efforts regretfully abandoned –
this recycled hay –
dried –
lit the fire for the meal of another day.*

*The sisters in this poem were sent by their mother to search for kindling in the streets of the small German town where they lived after WWII. The two girls and their parents were then refugees from a centuries-old German-speaking area in Yugoslavia, known then as Gottschee (today Kocevije in Slovenia). The sisters were utterly embarrassed about being shunned as refugees, and in addition being ordered to find and collect horse apples.

Photograph by Emma (nee Obwexer) Frener,
December 6th, 2020. Used with permission.
Photograph is in the author's inventory.

SOFT SNOW IN HESSE
(2018-2021)
*For Fenja Petschauer**

Fluffy snow bends green branches –
white wool warms for this cold February day.

A sudden wind gust lifts the blankets –
crystal flakes meet the snow-covered ground.

Branch after branch –
snaps back into place.

Winter surely will return another day.

Originally published in
Peter W. Petschauer, *Hopes and Fears: Past and Present*
(MindMend Publishing, 2019), p. 30. Slightly revised.

*Fenja is my granddaughter; she lives in Baden-Württemberg,
Germany.

William (Bill) Dunlap, *Mill Ridge,* 1970s (multimedia; 32" x 64").
Photograph by Peter W. Petschauer.
Original painting and photograph are in author's inventory.

SNOW SCENE
(2020-2021)
For William (Bill) Dunlap *

Bill Dunlap's winter scene hangs above –
a moment of the artist's reflection.
While snow covers the landscape,
the afternoon's reddish sky anticipates the end of another day.

Bitter cold pervades this creation.
As a reminder of this reality –
a few trees stand as if naked.
Someone cleared the long path to the house.

I sit by the fire on a late fall afternoon,
warmed by the sense of not walking in this scene.*

*William (Bill) Dunlap is a well-known artist and long-standing friend. Decades ago, he taught in the Art Department at Appalachian State University. We first met each other when his first wife attended one of my World Civilization classes and introduced us.

From
https://buddhaweekly.com/wp-content/uploads/matsuo-basho.jpg

NATURE

THREE SETS OF COLORS
(2017-2019)
*In honor of Matsuo Basho**

They sprang out of the ground yesterday –
against brown leaves.
Colors luminous and intense.

Crocus' tiny petals –
purple, yellow, white.
Frail and yet so strong –
they carried on after the morning's frost.

They make us smile and know,
these are bouquets of spring.

A bit early this year,
but undeterred.
They declare their persistence,
while curious bees discover their first reward.

From https://worldoffloweringplants.com/grow-care-crocus/

*Matsuo Basho was a Japanese poet who is best known in the West for his late 17th-century writings. Early on in my attempts with poetry, Matsuo Basho became my inspiration … even my students for years enjoyed some of Basho's unique poetry. See, for example, Matsuo Basho, translated Sam Hamill, *Narrow Road to the Interior and other Writings* (Boulder, 1998).

BORROWED VIEW
(2015-2021)

On the craggy cherry tree next door –
frail branches hold fluffy balls of white and pink.
Millions of petals dance above
the moss-covered roof just below.

Inspired fleeting moments.

Barely kissed by the warming sun,
the flowering glory ends.
Gentle breezes carry tiny flakes
to the ground.

Green leaves supplant the glory –
winter has departed.

*Originally published in Petschauer, *Hopes and Fears*, p. 31.
Slightly revised.

Appletree along the path in Erlstätt, Bavaria, Germany. Photograph by Peter W. Petschauer, Spring 2020. Photograph is in the author's inventory.

THE BEES ALONG THE PATH
(2020)

Next to the path up the hill,
bees are at work in a wild apple bush –
the humming of a thousand wings.
In their frenzied search for pollen,
they catapult each near the other –
from one petal to the next.
Their labor's fruit sticks to their legs –
for the hive's food and honeycombs.

Daffodils and crocus stand ignored.
Their turn is next,
if they are still in bloom when the tree drops its petals
and tiny apples emerge instead.

Yellow crocus. Photograph by Joni Webb
Petschauer, March 2019. Photograph is in the
author's inventory.

BAVARIAN SPRING
(2020)

Some flowers had lifted their tiny heads:
Purple and yellowish hues,
harbingers of spring.
Sitting outside once again,
cool beers and conversation flowed.
Surely winter will not return.

But the cold we missed then
now stormed in with uninhibited briskness.
No precipitation, just bitter wind.
Frail heads of flowers drooped,
bees' excursions to the cherry tree abandoned,
their soothing hum silenced by the sun's frosty rays.
We too retreated just in time.

The SARS-CoV-2 virus emerged simultaneous
to winter's reappearance.
Stay home, the order said –
Germany's Bavaria led the way and we followed suit.
Apprehensions and staying put –
we only ventured out alone and
with members of our family.
"Social-distancing" became the norm –
a new word combination suddenly in vogue.*
Collective memories of medieval strictures –
then it was the Pest.
Quarantine not new to Europe's
recollections or languages.

Why be outside anyway
in that bone-chilling cold?
Rather quarter inside and rediscover love or
yell out festering frustration.
Loving and fighting –
babies in nine months and divorces maybe sooner.

Spring in Bavaria.
The returning cold and the invasion of a virus –
hoarding food and oddly rationing
paper for the toilet.

Hang in there though:
Soothing warmth will return,
the virulent virus will abate,
flowers will recover,
bees will fly again and
we will sit outside in the sun.

Published *Clio's Psyche,* Spring 2020, 26 (3), pp. 287-288.
Published with permission. Slightly revised.

*The distance between two non-family members was to be 6 feet
or 1.5 meters.

A BABY CRYING*
(2019)

A baby crying incessantly –
not hearing birds in loud conversation –
unaware of green meadows spreading to the mountains.

Tiny flowers sprouting by the millions –
golden forsythias against blue skies –
red roofs against grayish trees.

A woman struggling with roots in her garden –
a girl training a horse in the roundabout –
a family enjoying a beer, or two, under an umbrella.
The sun is already strong.

Spring arrived in Bavaria early this year –
with hope in its ordinariness and excesses.

*This poem originated with an actual scene. A mother or
grandmother placed their baby in a convertible crib on their
balcony; after a time, the child became bored or hungry and
hollered for someone to pay attention to her.

A gnarled tree on the shore of Bavaria's Lake Chiem. Photograph by Peter W. Petschauer, April 30th, 2017. Photograph is in the author's inventory.

THE GNARLED TREE*
(2017-2020)

The gnarled tree stood all winter –
all alone.
One massive branch hung barely above the ground –
others reached unsteadily to the sky –
Loden moss clung to its surface.
The only visitor –
the howling Northwesterner.*

Soothing sunshine arrived with April –
diminutive flowers raised their daring heads –
verdant hillsides in refreshing green.
People walked outside again.

Petals sprang from the tree's every extremity,
the mighty branch weighed down further by their mass.
Eager visitors arrived in swarms –
bees discovered supplies for next winter and their keeper.

Their humming concert gave joy to passers-by
and the reassurance of another season to the aging tree.

*I did not take a photograph of the tree which inspired the poem
"The Gnarled Tree." Thus, this magnificent tree must serve as a
worthy substitute. BTW, in the Bavarian area, where we stayed,
the prevailing wind originates in the West.

A red Marin in Western Europe.
From: https://www..de/news/2019/10/27093.html

*On our walks near Erlstätt in Bavaria, my wife and I often watched several of these magnificent birds, the red Marins, circling above. The last line … it takes us beyond our own perceptions of the things for which a bird might look.

NATURE

I WISH I COULD FLY*
(2020)

I wish I could fly like the red Marin,
with wingspans wider than my arms
and split tail feathers to steer my way.
To lift my slender body,
with pectoral muscles strong as those in my arms.

But not with waxen appendages attached,
like Icarus, the young Greek,
who alighted from a cliff –
frenzied voices of prison guards behind him.
"The sun better not melt my wings,
should I rise too high and crash to the ground."

Soaring in the sky,
spying for mice and moles,
swooping down with torrid speed,
catching them in a moment of inattention,
discerning too late the danger descending from above.
This is one skill I would apply with abandon.

But coasting above would be my favorite time,
buoyed by thermal winds and enhanced by my lightness,
not wishing to walk or ride,
like the clumsy creatures on the ground:
slow on two legs or noisy on four wheels,
never with a meal for me.

LIFE

Gottfried Frener's photograph of February 20th, 2019 shows me nearing the 80 birthday in the Dolomite Mountains of Northern Italy. Photograph is in the author's inventory.

AT 80*
(2019-2020)
For all those who reach this honorable age

Eighty!
It feels like always –
until the mirror reflects the reality.
I'd rather be as young as I feel.

At 30, age 60 appeared an unattainable goal –
at age 45, being 75 was far in the distance, and
at age 70, it occurred to me only in passing to be alive at 80.
I hear of 90-year-olds thriving and driving brand new cars.
Do I want to be there?
How will I get there?

Thirty seems like yesterday –
some recollections drift further back.
I am a child on an alpine meadow sunning in soft rays.
Riding the subway in New York City,
studying European history.

I am in yesterday –
until I feel my body's aches.
The years collapse –
I am in the present –
an aging man.

We have no choice to whom we are born,
where we are born,
or even when we are born.
We have a choice with whom we share our trust and our time.
Family and friends are highest on the list.
What is else is there?
Wealth, cars, houses, clothes, and food?
All so fleeting without a community of others.

But there is genuine pleasure in,
"I am still here."

The joy of greeting the sun in the morning
and admiring its descent in the evening.

Its reddish hue predicting another sun-filled day.

There is walking along "our" favorite path,
looking out over "our" lake,
some days still as glass
others abundant with shimmering waves.
Then I feel as if the years had passed me by
                                        untouched.

Dr. Erich Petschauer greeting Archbishop Johannes Geisler for his signature on "The Day of the Option," 1940. Photographer is unknown; possibly Hildegard Petschauer who identified it on the back. Original is in the author's inventory.*

THE KNIFE
(2013-2020)
For those who wrestled with a parent's past

This knife is not made of steel,
yet it sits buried in my stomach –
every day a reminder of a past
not of my making.

This knife of thoughts and emotions,
now deeply ingrained.
I placed it there decades ago –
in realization of my father's loyalty to the NS regime.

His decision to join a government,
I rightly decry.

Without killing anyone,
he condoned the murder of millions in mayhem and in war,
inspired by leaders uncaring of the lives of others.

This knife is made of realizations,
thoughts which no child should have to bear –
covered with the blood of the original wounds.

The lives of others ended
with the vicious weapons of resentment and of hate.
Human beings cut down like rye in a field.

The knife in my innards
is the recognition of my father's acceptance
of the murder of human beings like he, you and me.

We might know the names of these others –
but not the futures of the innocent men and women,
children even,
who walked our streets and paths –
full of hopes and dreams.

This knife of awareness and anger,
at the loss of talent beyond compare
and with it –
music, literature, and art.

Were it I could accept my distance
from the original decision.
Knowing full well it was my father's choice –
not mine.

Then he thought to be correct.
We all know
he was wrong,
even if he wrote later that he knew it was.
But this recognition does not alleviate the pain.

Now though –
how to remove this pointed knife?

How to grant pardon –
having neither committed nor condoned a crime,
yet having to live with its nagging aftermath?

Die Option, the option, meant that the German/Austrian speakers of the former Austro-Hungarian territory of South Tyrol were asked/persuaded to opt to "Return home to the Reich" (Heim ins Reich). My father, Erich Petschauer, as the local representative of the Reich, encouraged Archbishop Johannes Geisler to "opt" to leave the area "with his flock."

Bath Abby, England. Photograph by Peter W. Petschauer,
September 2010. Photograph is in the author's inventory.

EVOLUTION'S EVOLUTION
(2020)
For Howard Stein

Knowing of an others' ailment
reminds me of my own aching body.
I understand now so clearly:
Your pain chains you to your declining frame –
as it does me to mine.
Illnesses that seemed so well controlled –
reawakened to inflict untold misery.

I once accepted without second thought
parts of the body through eons created
to support an ever-increasing brain –
women's widening pelvis –
accommodation to an infant's expanding head.

Eyes that savor a beautiful sunset,
may as well deliver the message
of the wreckage of a destructive war.

Ears that absorb soothing melodies of Mozart,
cannot block the jarring detonations of hand-grenades.

The mouth that soothes an infant's frail being
may issue an authoritarian's vilest commands.

Hands that lovingly caress the body of another,
that work with chisels and axes
to erect homes, churches, and palaces,
may turn and destroy them with dogged will.

Muscles we thought would bear us forever,
will give way to Newton's falling apple.

The brain, a beautiful fruition of creation
with untold ingenuity in its crevices,
may just as well participate in the undoing
of the carriage that underpins it.

Feet that lug our massive edifice
in support of our brain's exploration
of the furthest corners of our globe and universe
may turn into burdens when neuropathy aborts their purpose.

Still, the magnificence of this cranial vault
uplifts itself and others
who bear equal burdens of this evolutionary achievement.
The pain of aging brings serenity and wisdom.

The official wedding photograph of Maria (Moitz) (nee Clara) Mantinger and Gottfried (Fried'l) Mantinger. Photograph Planinschek, Brixen/Bressanone. Original photograph used with permission and is in the inventory of the Molser family.*

MOITZ AND HANS
(2020)
In honor of the Molser and Schölzhorn families

We buried Moitz
in the graveyard of S. Georg, our Baroque church.
For 230 years it embraced worshippers
high up in the Dolomites.
Forty kilometers away,
we interred Hans in the graveyard of the city's
even older Gothic edifice.
Neither church could have held more mourners.
Many stood,
the spaces to kneel filled completely.
She was two days shy of 93 –
he had just turned 68.

Maria was her given name –
we called her Moitz.
We grew up on the same "old" farm -
the toilet and cold water were outside,
we slept on straw sacks and
covered ourselves with feather beds –
they offered comfort in every season.
Four girls, one male servant, three children from farms
                         that had too many, my brother and I –
that was our farm.

She married the heir of another mountain farm.
For over three hundred years,
it offered survival to his family,
until her son preceded her to the graveyard a decade ago.
She lies with him in the cross-adorned family's resting place,
where her brother's image watches steadily
from the warriors' memorial.
Killed in Yugoslavia after the WWII –
his abused body never found.
Moitz' husband, the Molser farmer,
waited there for her as well.

She kept her mind to the very end,
even as her body sank into disarray.
I was "her brother,"
so she said.
The common history linking us beyond her death.

Barely three weeks had passed when death overtook Hans,
Johann, his name in the record books.
He married Moitz's oldest niece
and their home stands in a nearby city,
indoor plumbing and all.
He a plumber, she a nurse:
the rising urban middle class, one might say in academic circles.
The outdoors was his home –
climbed every mountain he could find
on five continents and skied with determined passion.

A wedding photograph of Johann (Hans) Schölzhorn and
Martina (nee Obwexer) Schölzhorn. Original photograph
used with permission and is in the inventory of Schölzhorn
family.

Died in his sleep after lunch –
feet crossed and arms on his chest.
His face peaceful –
not a worry in the world.
No one watched as he went.

Three choirs sang ancient songs for the dead
                                in our village church –
the same Moitz had sung for over sixty years.
This time a daughter held the baton.
Three priests officiated –
of those assembled in the church many took communion.

Glorious trumpets invited angels down to Hans' final mass.
The cathedral's soaring space filled with vibrant voices
and the familiar tones of a great nephew's accordion.
Two priests offered this high mass –
the sermon on point as anyone could ever hear.

Anticipated death in one case,
surprise and shock in the other.
A deadly harvest in our family.
And yet,
grand children and great-grand children alike,
almost unknowingly carry on its traditions –
in the reassuring cycle that never ends.

*Maria (Moitz) Mantinger was the last of four Egarter sisters who survived WWII. She married one of the most eligible bachelors in the village; Gottfried (Fried'l) Mantinger, who died a few years before her. She herself died a month after my wife Joni and I visited her in Afers/Eores, the village in which I grew up on the Egarter farm. This was shortly before COVID-19 restricted travel within Europe.

Johann (Hans) Schölzhorn was married to Moitz's niece Martina, the daughter of Agnes (Neas) Obwexer, Moitz's sister. Hans was a devoted athlete who climbed mountains and skied on every continent. He died unexpectedly in his sleep after a light lunch. My wife and I were able to attend his funeral mass and burial. A few days later, the border between Austria and Italy closed, and we could not see the family again before we left Europe in June 2020.

WOMEN AROUND ME
(1979-2020)

Going out to dinner,
turning in the bed at night,
waking in the morning.
Hiking in the mountains,
sunbathing at the shore,
children in tow.

Budding flowers,
receptive bodies,
heady lovers,
bewildered husbands,
rebellious offspring,
lined faces.

Beautiful, helping – helped
Bright, advising – advised
Absorbing, loving – loved
Sexy, manipulating – manipulated
Demanding, holding – held.

A stream of experiences:
Knowing one is knowing none,
being with one,
being with all.

Women, witches,
Women, whores,
Women, virgins,
Women, goddesses,
Women, equals.

Woman infinite,
women, women!

Ageless, eternal.

Melanie (Mele) Maria Petschauer as a child.
Photograph by Wade Evans.
Photograph is in the author's inventory.*

LOSING MY DAUGHTER
(1978-2021)
For Melanie Petschauer

Sometimes I see you on the lawn –
in the grass.
Sometimes I hear you in the bedroom –
laughing and crying.
Sometimes I feel you holding onto me –
in nameless fear.
Yes, sometimes you seem so very near.

You loved me without adult constraint –
you waited for me all too often without complaint.
You had no doubt about our world.
And you were not of our hidden troubles told.

Now you are nearly out of my life –
strife tore apart what was once our home,
but my memories of you remain.

The moments together now are all too fleeting –
few new memories come with all this parting.
I miss the most beautiful word:
"Daddy."
I see you rarely now, my baby –
grown, with your own young daughter.

Old flashes running through my mind,
that's all I usually find.
Forgive me,
if my love is nearly blind.
But be assured,
memories are kind –
thankfully.

*Wade Evans took the photograph before Melanie's mother and
she moved to Germany. The photo was taken in Boone, NC.

Dr. Alois Alzheimer after whom the disease is named.
Photograph is available on Internet at
histooir_jaune03_img01.jpg.*

UMNACHTUNG (NIGHT FALLING)
(2020-2021)
In honor of the women in the extended family
who succumbed to one of these brutal maladies

Names and events vanish from my mind –
no way to ignore this brutal fact.
Sentences disappear like pages
torn from the brain's most private diaries,
like words and memories,
that once told me the meaning of a text.
Telling stories over and over of times since forgotten,
yet not remembering the lunch consumed with gusto yesterday.
Functioning at daily tasks like a pro,
yet unable to recall which way to turn a spent bulb
to replace it with a fresh one.

Family members not talking to me,
the patient,
of the calamity before them.
Asking behind my back,
with that concerned tone:
"How is she doing?"
"Today is a good day, she remembers my name."
"Any hope for improvement?"
"Improvement?
Every day is different,
with spurts of remissions and relapses in random order."
"Good God, a year ago, she was this brilliant woman."
"Don't tell her about night moving in –
she is not aware of it."

My remnant mental capacities scream in frustrated dismay:
I know what's going on.
This is the sunset:
meadows gradually darken,
trees reluctantly relinquish the pink of the sun's last rays.
It is the arrival of the night as dementia,
or Dr. Alois Alzheimer's far more serious calamity –
as it overwhelms my brain with scars and plaques.

You are the fools who don't admit what troubles me.
This once excellent mind,
unable to defend this person who once was I,
or to end its misery.

* Dr. Alzheimer was a German clinical psychiatrist and neuroanatomist, who lived and worked in several contemporary clinical settings. His discoveries go back to the outset of the last century. Read more here:
https://www.ncbi.nlm.nih.gov/pmc/articles/PMC3181715/

A Woman in similar attire to one in the author's dream.*

NIGHTTIME VISITOR
(2018-2020)
For all those who were tortured by dreams such as these

She arrived in a rush of freezing air
in the depth of night.
Ripped me from my sleep.
Nowhere to hide.
Pull up the covers!

She stood at the foot of my bed,
staring far ahead.
Her back as straight as a board,
tall, slender,
middle-aged.
Gray hair protruding beneath her bonnet.

White lace around her high collar and the ends of her sleeves.
Silk mesh over her décolletage.
Long gloves held in her right.

She came in July 1993 –
from the 1890s.
This black mirage.

This in the former house of prostitution,
or long since so rumored,
the one with screw-spikes and balls on its iron-rod fence.

The soft voice broke the silence:
"Release me from my tomb,
my girls are gone.
I am without my place.
I am so very cold.
Release me.
PLEASE,
release me."

No response necessary or given.
She left as quickly as she had arrived.
Right there, in the middle of the College.
Teeth ceased chattering -
warmth returned to the room.
My fear abated.

*I discovered this photograph on
Skinnerinc.com/auctions/2570M/lots/718. "Portrait of a Dark-
haired Woman Wearing a Black Dress (c. 1845). Unsigned. Oil
on board, 19 1/2 x 16 1/2 in., in a period gilt-stenciled painted
wood frame. Condition: Craquelure, scattered retouch."

FORGET
(2020)

We forget because we must.
Without forgetting we cannot function
and function we must
for our children, lovers, and parents.
We cannot forget
because we become useless to ourselves
and to the others.

We work as if obsessed to forget
and lose our families and friends –
the time for them evaporates.
We play to excess to avoid thinking about the pain,
yet it glares at us in the midst of our supposed delight.
We imbibe alcohol until it troubles us no more,
except the next morning,
when our head thumps in its unique fashion –
we drink more to overcome the ache.
We consume drugs at any time of day –
until we are addicted and cease to function.

So many ways to fool ourselves when we need
to confront the validity of our wound!
The father who beat us –
The uncle who raped us –
The business partner who cheated us –
The mother who left us –
The political party who betrayed itself and us.
The god whom we thought on our side -
no more than a collection of past explanations.
If we wait until it's too late to face the hurt –
frailty may overwhelm the body and mind
and silence us forever.

We can only hope –
our memory lingers in those who survive us.

The composer Gustav Mahler. Austrian Photographer (early 20th century). Marke: KUNTKOPIE.DE.*

OTHER TIMES
(2019-2020)
For Joni Petschauer

The smell of fresh-cut grass –
a mountain farm's yard,
leaps of freshly shorn sheep.
A massive cloudburst drumming on a gable –
a shingled roof in the plains,
here and there water dripping to the floor.
The whiff of a polished table –
monthly waxing of the staircase,
our servant's aching back.
The gentle fragrance of lilac –
a garden in a castle,
hopes of a scoop of strawberry ice cream.
The pungent odor of mold in an antique store –
a museum in Venice,
mold creeping upward on Titian's paintings.
The sound of wind in my ears –
a windswept mountain at 9500 feet,
a rising sun painting pink persistent clouds.
A small plane flying overhead –
warplanes screaming in the blue sky of October 1944,
sprinting under a tree in total fright in July 1954.
Mozart in the background of my computer –
a sweltering auditorium in St. Petersburg,
the full orchestra and choir rendering Mahler's *Auferstehung*.
Squeals of a car turning at top speed –
the corner down the street,
nightly shrill noises of the streetcar.
Water running in the kitchen –
stacks of dishes in the tiny sink,
washing postponed all too long.
The touch of a piece of refined woolen cloth –
a sweater emerging magically,
my favorite childhood woman with her knitting needles.
The most stunning woman on a train –
my girlfriend on the ferry,
homeward bound to Staten Island.

My father and I in an odd dream
conversing in his living room,
alerting me of his approaching death.
The wafting aroma of fresh coffee –
an Italian machine fizzing loudly in a café,
my mother waiting for her favorite beverage.
The noises of a meal emerging –
my wife in the kitchen,
taste buds recalling previous refined feasts.

Tentacles of other times
reaching into the present.
The illusion of being young forever.

Notes (fragment) for Mahler's Symphony No. 2
"Resurrection" (*Auferstehung*) – from the Internet

*Gustav Mahler became one of my favorite composers after I heard
the Austrian's brilliant Symphony #2, *Auferstehung*, in the
Philharmonia in St. Petersburg, Russia.
(https://en.wikipedia.org/wiki/Saint_Petersburg_Philharmonia)

During the several summers when Joni and I taught in an international
summer institute in Olomouc, CZ, we regularly visited Cafe Mahler,
down the street from Mahler's domicile.
(https://www.tripadvisor.de/Restaurant_Review-g274718-d2571854-
Reviews-Cafe_Mahler-Olomouc_Olomouc_Region_Moravia.html)

Church bells. From https://pixabay.com/de/photos/glocken-kirchenglocken-leuten-5019971/.

LIFE SOUNDS
(2016)
*For Sabrina Marchioro and Walter Frenzel**

The clatter of three horses' hoofs
below a window.
A small town in Bavaria.

The bells of a Baroque church
in the mountains of Northern Italy.

The screeching of a streetcar on the corner
in the middle of the night.
A city in the Rhineland.

The scratching of a mouse
on the plastic liner of a garbage can.
The house on Grand Boulevard.

The voices of colleagues
in the department.
A university in the Appalachian Mountains.

The transparency of Antonio Vivaldi's violins
as if played once more.
Venice right here now.

The clicking of a computer's keyboard
in many places
around the globe.

Falling asleep
regular thumping of two hearts.

The soft breathing of my beloved partner
in a shared bed.

Reassurances of life.

First published in Petschauer, *Hopes and Fears,* p. 22. Slightly revised.

*My wife Joni and I rented from the Marchioro/Frenzel family in Erlstätt every winter since 2010.

SOFT VOICES
(2015)
In honor of Denise Ringler

Voices
on the bus –
soft and reassuring.
Undisturbed by the motor's hum.

A conversation with a friend
in seats next to each other.
Warm moments of intimacy.

Then …
Arrival and goodbyes.

INVISIBLE*
(2018)
In honor of Radio City Music Hall's Rockettes

Visible,
but not seen:
An elevator boy many decades ago.

As if a servant of another time –
part of the machinery.
Uninhibited conversations all around.

A threatening voice.
"Are you listening?"
"Not really, no."

Here comes another floor.
"Going up?"
"Yes."

Published in
Petschauer, P. (2020). *An Immigrant in the 1960s. Finding Hope
and Success in New York City.* Perspektiven Presse. (p. 56)
Slightly revised.

*I was a backstage elevator operator in RCMH for a few months
in 1967.

Portrait of Johann Sebastian Bach by Elias Gottlieb
Haussmann. Images from
https://en.wikipedia.org/wiki/Johann_Sebastian_Bach.

BACH-ALIA
(2013-2020)

Your notes flew across the pages –
your hands and feet raced across keys and pedals,
as if by magic.
Page after page.

Your notes created melodies –
your voices soared to heaven's door
as if by magic.
Sunday after Sunday.

Your rhythms had not been heard before –
your texts brought joy even without a sound,
as if by magic.
Week after week.

They did not know you to be unique.
Even later interpreters fall short in grasping
your flights of genius,
dear Johann Sebastian.

Kantate zum 27. Sonntag nach Trinitatis
Cantata for 27. Sunday after Trinity

Wachet auf, ruft uns die Stimme
Wake ye maids! hark, strikes the hour

BWV 140

J. S. Bach – Cantata BMV 140 "Wacht auf ruft uns die Stimme"

A colleagues' library. Photograph by Peter W.
Petschauer, 2017. Image is used with permission.
Photograph is in the author's inventory.

ODE TO BOOKS
(2018-2019)
For Peter and Petra Lange

On display in homes of the wealthiest
and in teachers' humble abodes.
Read avidly by corporate executives,
advising on the net the ones they recommend.
Still required reading in classes on occasion,
a list for those loyal to the written word.

Almost forgotten in splendid edifices –
they hide patiently in libraries built many decades ago.
We search via Google now.

Yet there they are –
companions in the subway, on a train, in a bus.
Folks reading on the way to and from their place of work.

Sometimes on a plane –
someone chasing to a meeting far away.
Or to while away the time in the doctor's office –
infinite hours of waiting.
More rarely still at the beach –
in a humble bag in the company of cool drinks.

Houses rarely now built to make room for books:
"They clutter the place, they collect dust."
Space allotted to screens –
entertainment without much thought.

Politicians rarely spotted with a book in hand,
inconvenient truths may await on its pages.
Loss of dignity in the halls of power –
our species' deadly evolutionary track –
the loss of creatures not as adaptable –
ice sheets melting on poles and mountains.

Once proudly read and applied by the educated and the aspiring.
Collected in Alexandria long before Gutenberg's invention.
Often disdained today by those who would do well to read them
as they attempt to guide us.

The remnants of a couple's art collection.
Photograph by Peter W. Petschauer, 2010.
Photograph is in the author's inventory.

SEPARATION'S HIGH COST*
(2016-2019)

Crumbled paper,
cardboard separators,
plastic wrapping –
all strewn about the container.
The floor covered with cruddy litter.

Art stored in flimsy boxes –
paintings torn from wrappings –
canvases without their frames –
frames without their content.

Surely robbers' dirty work.

Broken promises instead,
deserted and unloved.

Musty smells pervading,
sticky dust having settled in.

Art as an investment.
Art as a source of recognition.
Then too,
art for itself.
Essentials of a culture.

Boasters and auctioneers –
not robbers tore apart lofty aspirations.

Orphaned art bemoaning lost attachments
                                            and significance.

*My dismay is less with the divorce and the later death of the husband than the mistreatment of their art by one of the major auction houses in North Carolina. To this day, I do not comprehend how the staff of a well-reputed establishment could mistreat art so callously. I have broken all contact with it.

From Dreamstime. Stock photo.

THE BUREAUCRAT
(1978-2019)

Another day!
Eyes hurting,
head aching,
limbs moving slowly.
It must be morning.

Running!
Cold carpet, hot water –
Irish soap, Brazilian coffee –
crisp toast with marmalade –
assorted news –
foggy windows, gray pavement.

All in a Day!

Mail's steady flow –
efficient memoranda –
urgent messages –
fruitful meetings.

Working!
Assistants, smiles –
chairs, conversations –
staffers, decisions –
regulations, compromises.

More in a Day!
Scarce resource allocations –
following prescribed routines –
allowing no exceptions –
keeping files correctly.

Worn to the bone!
Cool air, pushing crowds –
solid car, weary poolers –
cutting grass, nagging kids –
soft bed, softer woman.

What happened to Ms. Doing's letter?
Did she demand an exception?
How about Mr. Super in the corner office,
did he like the joke?

The Giant's Remains. Photograph by Peter W. Petschauer, February 17th, 2021. Photograph is in the author's inventory.

THE GIANT IN THE FOREST*
(2018-2020)

A tiny seed fell into the gulley.
Leaves covered it –
the fertile soil embraced it –
a nearby spring nourished it –
older trees protected it.

A giant rose from this humble start –
its roots reached deep into the ground.
The wind played music in its generous branches –
birds made their nests deep inside –
squirrels found their home.
Saplings grew in its shadow –
relied on its protection.

One summer,
the spring dried up –
deep cracks tore through the gully.
The giant's needles drooped listlessly.

Relief came with steady rain.
Animals, plants, and trees chatted joyously –
the spring bubbled once again –
the gulley's cracks filled with water.
Thick sap arose in the giant's trunk –
its needles perked up again.

A fierce storm arose one night.
Unrelenting spray swept into every hiding place
under the forest's canopy.
The giant felt its roots loosen from the soil –
the perfect spot that sustained it so well.

Its moans called out to friends and neighbors.
They held out their branches –
swayed in rhythmic understanding.

To no avail!
The giant leaned forward,
lost its balance and swooshed to the ground.
It took along the others who came to its aid.
The crash reverberated through the forest –
birds and squirrels shaken from their dreams,
as were the deer.

The giant's roots stand exposed –
sun, rain, and snow washing off the soil –
its top cut away.
Cars had precedence on the road where it fell.

A sapling stands bent in the fallen tree's remains –
another giant's life has sprouted.

*I came across the massive Ponderosa pine the day after it toppled. It broke my heart to see such a beautiful tree fall, and to be cut within the hour, so that a car could pass on the road below the path to Bass Lake, NC. It was part of a cluster of Ponderosas that grow straight up without branches until they spread them at about 70, or more, feet.

TWO GARDENS, WORLDS APART
(2017-2020)

Among steep, red-tiled roofs,
two worlds apart and yet so near.

A worn wall –
five feet tall, six inches wide –
gray tiles over stained white paint.

Here –
a rambling German garden:
designed decades ago, maybe before the war.
Brown slippery dirt its most prominent feature.
Stones arranged by another generation –
today strewn about in disarray.
A massive tulip tree in a corner –
petals falling on overgrown paths.

There –
a trim Japanese garden –
lovingly arranged.
On its borders and in bloom graceful and manicured:
Forsythias, tulips, and punctatums.
A terracotta Buddha guards a birdbath in freshly-cut grass.
A white globe symbolizes a wider world.

Sparrows unaware of human borders –
nest in the creations of past and current gardeners.

Photograph by Peter W. Petschauer, November 13th, 2018. Photograph is in the author's inventory.

MOON BOATS
(2018-2019)
For John and Ana Shellem

A ghostly presence –
the full moon above.

Rippling waves on glistening water.

Sailboats swaying –
ropes clanking in rhythm on their masts.

TROUBLES

Titian's portrait of the older Charles V, the Holy Roman
Emperor. Courtesy of Kunsthistorisches Museum, Vienna.*
From https://www.habsburger.net/en/media/tiziano-vecellio-
titian-emperor-charles-v-armour-mid-16th-century-0

*I chose to use Charles V's portrait because he inherited the massive
empire that literally stretched from one end of the then known world
to the other. His son Phillip II is best known in our part of the world
for the Armada that he launched against England and failed; it was
not this failure though that destroyed his empire. It had grown too
large to rule by one man from one center.

ALL-POWERFUL EMPIRES
(2020)
For Paul Elovitz

We know the cycle:
Empires start out small –
a few exceptions shore up the rule.
Then quickly,
tenaciously they expand –
become vast territorial accumulations.
Shrewd leadership,
long-term goals,
military innovations,
these push them to the fore.

Most collapse in internal tumult or a whimper.

Caesar Augustus remade the Republic –
senators called him divine and *imperator*.
His family solidified the authoritarian trend –
even if the *Pretorians* ended its existence.
Nero was the *imperator* they murdered.
But the family had started a tradition:
The *Imperium Romanum,*
the Empire we study to this day.
Ingenious leadership,
military innovation,
clever manipulation of enemies, and
internal recoveries –
they made for world domination.
North Africa and Spain, England and
the Middle East –
the emperor ruled them all.
Its roads and aqueducts admired still –
SPQR the recognizable symbol –
Latin lingers in our languages.
Rome fell to internal dissent, corruption,
family disputes, and military defeats.

Muscovy rose from a hunting cottage in the woods.

Then and now –
the Moskva River at its center.
Princes started their mission to rule the region –
shrewd autocrats succeeded one another,
never missed the goal.
Buying and selling,
marrying princesses near and far,
subduing self-important nobles –
all of this, they did so well.
Held together from Moscow and St. Petersburg –
the leaders did not think they would ever fail.
Corruption and overextension
tore it all down in WWI.

Ideology and inhumanity leadership started it up again.

A warlord started
this massive array of states –
known to us as the Mongolian.
It stretched from the Black Sea to the Pacific -
fell as quickly as it had arisen.
Only historians remember its unspeakable brutality
and its brilliant administration –
a few Russian words remind of its presence.
Family dissent and integration into Chinese culture –
they stopped this meteoric rise.

His empire devolved from his father Charles –
Phillip II, the son's name.
Educated and sophisticated,
bureaucratic innovations hold sway to this day.
Rule by subject category,
not by territory –
that was his idea.
In his vast holdings the sun never set –
Spanish spoken from Atlantic to Pacific.
Inheritance rules,
religious dissension, and
an expanse beyond one dynast's ability to command.
All these and more removed it from the map.

TROUBLES

This state started in a castle above Meran,
the city in South Tyrol –
as the place was known then and it is still known today.
History recalls the empire that arose as Austria-Hungary.
Its rulers, the Habsburgs,
harvested in every corner of middle Europe.
Marriage was their most effective tool –
war did not suit the family's approach.
But alliances that assisted its assent
lured it into catastrophe
and tore it down in that "war to end all wars."

We call them Pilgrims to this day –
the boat people from other shores.
They displaced native populations with armor and deceit.
Became a major power through revolution,
Innovations, and so-called purchases of land.
It too stretches from Atlantic to Pacific.
Corruption,
internal dissent, and
external wars are tearing it apart:
Authoritarianism is its major trap.

Each empire's miscalculation –
that it will never disappear:
Arrogance but one of many flaws –
overextension still another –
corruption never absent.
Underestimating enemies,
a psychological misunderstanding.
Foes copying military innovations
and family feuds rarely absent from disaster.

Are we learning from this accumulation of lessons?

History offers this resounding answer:
"You have the singular capacity
to ignore the lessons of the past."

The Pergamon Museum in Berlin, Germany. From Berlin.de.

CREATING IMAGES
(2020-2021)

An ancient king ascended a hilltop temple –
surrounded by his nobles.
He offered what they deemed appropriate –
but the gods left him without assurance.

A pharaoh followed by his afterbirth –
an indication of his godlike presence.
He did not rest undisturbed in his tomb –
robbers stripped it of the necessities for afterlife.

A Roman senator in his Muslim toga –
hosted guests to an obligatory party.
They snickered behind his back –
knowing what the show was all about.

A Mongol king in stunning attire atop a splendid steed –
obviously situated above all others.
His horse stumbled and ended the charade –
no one rushed to his aid as the king struggled in the mud.

A European noble in steely attire –
reminding scions and peons of his prowess.
A lance threw him sideways –
he lay there struggling like a turtle overturned.

Louis XIV's princely attendants genuflected around his bed –
the rising sun backdrop to his altar.
Their sullen faces an indication of the stink –
it arose not just from the royal pot.

The Russian tsar surrounded by Orthodox dignitaries –
a seeming affirmation that he spoke daily with his God.
The soldiers on the Western Front smirked at the audacity –
enemy soldiers had overrun their positions.

Hitler in his palace with his architect –
plans for the capital of his thousand-year reign
                                    weighed down a nearby table.

Germany's soldiers could have stayed warm in a heated tent –
as they froze on the Eastern front.

Hundreds of flags fluttering in the breeze –
shored up the image of the empowered leader.
Followers accede to an authoritarian who sells himself adroitly –
even if his words are not followed by his actions.

Symbols readily understood by the many –
and all too readily abused by the few.
When the many recognize the deceit,
will it be too late to avert disaster?

Photograph by Hans Josef Domsta.
Original is in Domsta's possession.
Used with permission.

THE RETURN OF THE AUTHORITARIANS (2020)
For Hans Josef Domsta*

At the end of World War Two,
that horrific torture visited on humankind,
the authoritarians were wiped from the stage:
Mussolini and Hitler,
Pilsudski and Horthy.
The world breathed a sigh of relief.
With these meanest of mean men
and their intimates disappeared more than
seventy five years ago –
their arrogance in full display in their defeat.
They had suffered from their fathers' vicious hands –
learned at home to duck and to grovel
and readily succumb to their new masters' sway.**

Democracy spread across the globe –
ignoring a few holdovers from that other time:
Josef Stalin and Mao Zedong –

flag bearers to successor authoritarians.
Here they are again,
these self-centered men –
in places where they roosted once before:
Russia, China, Hungary, Poland.
Add long-standing democracies to the mix:
India and the United States.
And others,
hardly new to the experience:
Türkiye, Syria, Egypt and many more.
The misery of SARS-CoV-2 -
the excuse to strengthen their hold on power.

Psychologists, historians, and journalists recognize the type –
they have confronted him before.
Some members of the public too are aware of the bullies –
they relive their abusive households every day.

Once more pretty slogans cover the evil underneath:
Reactivating glorious pasts that rarely were;
browbeating political parties to their will;
pressuring reluctant parliaments to their side;
undermining institutions that restrain their kind;
stifling jurists' thoughtful voices;
ridiculing, jailing, killing even,
journalists who question their approach.

To jubilating followers –
these men represent their needs,
but they misinterpret the farce.
Authoritarians are about themselves
and their reach for glory –
not the men and women who hoist them into power.
Once more as well –
sycophants genuflect,
like their forebears –
their frail egos strong enough to feast,
like locusts on the fertile land.

Published in *The Journal of Psychohistory,* Fall 2020, 48 (2), pp. 163-164. Published with permission. Slightly revised.

*Dr. Domsta was my classmate first in Euskirchen, Germany, and then in Exaten, near Roermond in the Netherlands. He was city archivist for decades in Düren, Germany, and has written extensively about his region, including its sacred vessels, silver, and glass collections.

**Research shows that every one of Adolf Hitler's assistants grew up abused. Sven Fuchs, *Childhood is Political. War, Terror, Extremism, Dictatorships as Consequence of Destructive Childhood Experiences* (German; Mattes Verlag, 2019).

Lower Manhattan, New York City. Photograph by Peter W. Petschauer, from the Empire State Building, Fall 2012. Photograph is in the author's inventory.

CLOUD SCRAPER
(2018)
*For Susan Hein**

Repeat!
Repeat!
Repeat again!

The needle scrapes the clouds –
a response to the destruction of 9/11.
Taller than other giants around it –
visible for miles.
Even in the fog of downtown Manhattan –
it stands as testimony to the innocent deaths of that day.

But it and its neighbors
tempt the gods with their arrogance –
maleness in steel, glass, and concrete,
all symbols of a patriarchy!

Already the ancient Greeks knew –
jealous gods upend Hubris' foolish expressions.
Achilles,
quintessential hero of his time –
godlike in his mother Thetis' fibrous armor.
Apollo guided Paris' arrow to its weakest spot.

Ignoring our mothers' prescient concerns –
we moderns build
ever more audacious emblems of our maleness.
Surely they, too, will be torn asunder
by agents of other patriarchs.

Repeat!
Repeat!

And ignore the past!

Published in *Clio's Psyche*, Fall 2018, 25 (1), p. 125.
Published with permission.

*Susan Hein is an independent scholar and analyst in New York
City. She is an editor of *The Journal of Psychohistory* and is the
late Lloyd deMause's wife.

THE TYRANT'S DEATH
(2021)
For David Beisel

His cold hands lost the grip on power –
his abuses had caught up with him.
His obsequious sycophants cheered the guards –
they smothered him to death.

Throngs of people lined the streets as he was carried to his
eternal rest.
Behind him the praetorians with stone-faced mien –
orders he gave them shining on their chests.
His assistants with knowing smiles –
guilt not discernible on any of their faces.

Crowds cheered wildly as the cortège moved along –
one group taking up the joyful cry from the other.
Throughout the land people danced in the streets –
they'd lived to see the end of the monstrous regime.
Never again, they told each other.
Never,
ever!

He barely lay in his crypt with doors sealed tight –
when his children and disciples rose like springtime flowers.
They grabbed the reins of power without hesitation –
the very ones they ripped from him
in coldblooded murder.

The crowds who cheered the authoritarian's demise
suppressed thoughts of the new group's link to his oppression.
They argued to each other:
the old regime was not so bad –
surely this new group will not replicate
the worst abuses of the man they so despised.

"New" was an incorrect description
of the men and women who succeeded this authoritarian.
They usurped him to create their own regime –
in new clothes theirs was the old reborn.

They felt no hesitation to spread his kind of misery –
and to do so with unmeasured glee.

Published first in *Clio's Psyche*, Fall 2021, 28 (1), pp. 16-17.
Published with permission.

National Socialists destroyed the Jewish Cemetery in
Michelstadt, Hesse, Germany, in November 1938. Photograph
by Peter W. Petschauer, Spring 2019. Photograph is in the
author's inventory.

KILLING US*
(2019)
For Zohara Boyd

They kill with deeply felt emotion:
Fellow humans are their targets.

Carefully planned attacks:
Weapons meant for war,
and perfect spots for murder.
Schools, churches, theatres, shopping malls –
suited best to execute their prey.

Nefarious wordsmiths updating content:
Ideologies created for earlier times.
Mesmerized followers on TV, on the internet, and
men holding instruments of mass destruction.

The Second Amendment:
Lauded, derided, and misinterpreted –
our world of all or nothing.
Conservatives versus liberals,
small towns versus big cities,
and red versus blue.
Strident voices rise to a national cacophony –
block action that could stop the slaughter.

Published *Clio's Psyche*, Fall 2019, 26 (1), p. 95.
Published with permission. Slightly revised.

*My wife Joni and I visited this cemetery again in February 2022, with our granddaughter, and thought not only of Professor Zohara Boyd and the many family members killed by Nazis in Poland, but also of all the others who were murdered during the Holocaust. The destruction of cemeteries like this one in Michelstadt was another way for National Socialists to wipe out the memory of the very existence of Jews in this and many other towns. The hatred that divides our country today is hopefully not a precursor of such devastation in the U.S. The fate of Michelstadt's Jews is caught in Martin Schmall, *Die Juden in Michelstadt* (1988).

Max Halberstadt's famous photograph of Sigmund Freud.
Undated and in the Spanenthal Collection in England.
From https://shmh.de/en/max-halberstadt.

REPETITION COMPULSION
(2020)

Wiederholungszwang Sigmund Freud defined it
more than a century ago in Vienna –
repetition compulsion psychologists still call it
in English today –
destiny neurosis Erik Erickson surmised it
to be –
the rhythm of rise and fall of nations historians
named this inevitable repetition.

This behavior humans learn with little effort:
repeat and repeat again.
And feel perfectly well with their choices –
not even noticing they are there.
The student praised for the English essay
writes and writes again.
We know her as a novelist today.
The girl who lied to her mother about what
she and the teen did on the backseat of the car.
She learned to lie for life.
The boy who bullied another in school –
he bullied ever since.
The lover who found fault in his beloved's toe –
endeavored to find a better one in every lover,
over and over again.

A guard in Auschwitz who discovered pleasure
when first he beat an inmate –
promptly repeated the abuse every day.
Egypt's pharaohs thought success resides
in marriage within the family –
they continued the approach dynasty after dynasty,
in spite of evidence to the contrary.

The Stock Market ascends and descends,
no news there –
some investors though blithely ignore these cycles
                                        to their dismay,
like water in sand they see funds disappearing…

The military commander who succeeded once –
fearlessly attacks again and again –
the results on full display in the trenches of France,
the mountains of Afghanistan, and the cities of Ukraine.

Nations that design the perfect system for their success –
rarely succumb to their external foes.
Their internal divisions tear them down.

What we see in the mirror
usually is not what hides behind the glass.

ONE AMONG MANY*
(2020)

Among many in the bay,
two mighty flags –
one flew for America,
the other for Donald Trump.

The blue flag for "Trump 2020"
flew higher than the one of the United States.
Surely the man who hoisted them was unaware
of the proposition:
Trump trumping our very nation.

Does this unique positioning
serve the purpose of announcing that –
should he have won again,
he would have established the UST?

For all his enthusiasm, though,
the flag raiser in the boat was surely unaware –
he was alone with his demonstration of two
                              contradictory flags.

*I observed these flags in the bay off Wrightsville Beach, NC.

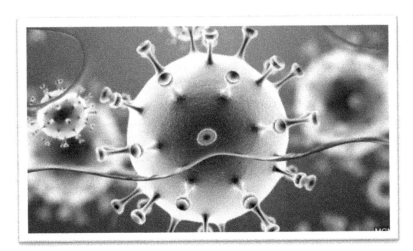

From https://www.publicdomainpictures.net/

DEATH BY COVID-19*
(2020)
In Memory of Lloyd deMause

By the middle of July 2020,
over 150,000 Americans fell victim to Covid-19.
Soon,
some statistics say,
thousands more will die.
By the time this tragedy runs its course –
hundreds of thousands will succumb.
Close to four million have been wounded,
now called the "infected."
This is a disaster some call a war.

Other wars –
an uncomfortable comparison
because fewer died:
25,000 lost in the Revolutionary War –
51,000 in Gettysburg –
58,209 in Vietnam –
36,516 in Korea –
and so far
6,626 in Iraq and Afghanistan.
9/11 bad enough,
yet then, too,
somewhat less than 3,000 succumbed.

Our commander-in-chief
rarely accepted ideas from his aides –
in this latest encounter,
called scientists and doctors.
His thoughts of genius utterly misplaced
and relying on his gut -
an uncertain guide.

History teaches relentlessly:
a commander not listening leads to defeat.
Just ask Hector, prince of Troy's mighty citadel,
or Xerxes, the arrogant Persian King,
or Hannibal, the brilliant Carthaginian scion,
or Robert E. Lee of "Southern" renown,
or Hitler, destroyer of his own Thousand-Year Reich.

Success rewards those who listen:
recall India's Emperor Ashoka,
or Ramses, the Great Egyptian pharaoh,
or Caesar Augustus, Rome's first emperor,
or Carolus Magnus of the Carolingian line,
or Ulysses Grant, who accepted the "Southern" general's sword,
or Eisenhower, of the Allied Forces' deserved fame,
or Merkel, wise chancellor in Central Europe.

Even if uninformed, disorganized, and spiteful –
loyal troops follow their commander to their doom.
Too many lie buried
on too many battlefields
and in graveyards across the globe.
Too late for them to realize –
their prideful chief ended there as well.

Published in *Clio's Psyche*, 27 (1) (Fall 2020), pp. 65-67.
Published with permission. Slightly modified.

*I wrote the poem before the death toll of COVID-19 had risen beyond 400,000 Americans during the winter of 2021. By the spring of 2022, more than 1,021,580 had died. (https://www.worldometers.info/coronavirus/#countries)

Lloyd deMause was a leading psychohistorian who developed a theory about the positive progression of the rearing of children from Ancient Times to the present. The title of this breakthrough essay is "The Evolution of Childhood." It may be found in Lloyd deMause, *Foundations of Psychohistory* (1982), pp.1-83.

WHY IT TROUBLES ME SO
(2019-2021)
*In Memory of Steve Feinstein**

It troubles me so!
We experienced it before, in my lifetime,
when totalitarians ruled the land.
This emergence of hating Jews.
Please, not twice in the very place
that attempted to banish this shadow side!
Many thousands forced
to leave the homes of their forebears.

Hundreds of thousands driven from
their life-giving work.
Mothers, sisters, daughters, grandmothers.
Mathematicians, physicians, chemists,
historians, psychologists, artists, musicians.

View of the railcar on display in the Permanent
Exhibition of the United States Holocaust Memorial
Museum. Washington DC, June 19th, 1991. Courtesy
of Polskie Koleje Panstwow S.A. It is a type of
Deutsche Reichsbahn car with which Jewish prisoners
were brought to concentration camps.

Thousands upon thousands chased from
their villages and towns – to their deaths.

Hundreds of thousands stuffed in trains.

Hot, standing, afraid, without food or latrines.
Men, women, children.
Herded to die in chambers
that spewed gas, not water.
Forced to disrobe before others
whom they knew only by their attire.
Those who appeared healthy,
selected to live longer – worked to death later.

Six million European Jews murdered –
Germans the initiators, others willing assistants:
Poles, Czechs, French, Dutch, Russians, Ukrainians
denied later all too often their vicious crimes.

Not for a moment should our generation
deny,
contemplate,
tolerate,
let alone commit itself to such terror once again.

Published in *Clio's Psyche*, 26 (2) (Winter 2020), p. 259. Published
with permission. Slightly revised.

*Dr. Steve Feinstein was my classmate at New York University in
the 1960s. He taught for 30 years at the University of Wisconsin at
River Falls; after his retirement in 1999, he established a thriving
Holocaust and Genocide Studies Center at the University of
Minnesota. He died after giving a presentation at a Jewish Film
Festival at the university. He spoke at my invitation at Appalachian
State University several years before then and used the image of a
RR car like the one shown above to make a point. Details about his
life at https://www.uwrf.edu/HIST/About/FacultyStaff/ Emeriti
StephenFeinstein.cfm.

The poem was conceived in Dr. Howard Stein's poetry workshop at
the International Psychohistory Association's meeting, May of 2019.

The balcony of the *Bayrischer Hof.* Image from the Hotel's
Website: https://www.bayerischerhof.de/de/

BACK IN *BAYERISCHER HOF**
(2015-2019)

You know you are there –
if you did not know already –
Mercedes, Ferraris, and Bentleys.
The sweetness of the perfume.
The rush of excitement so near the very best.

Men in suits – expensive, handmade suits.
Women in dresses –
haut couture from Paris and Milan.
Except on the terrace.
There they lounge in the hotel's white robes,
sipping champagne or cappuccino.

Mercedes drove up then too.
Diplomats, military, and SS –
they filled the halls.
Fine cut uniforms –
boots and belts to match.
Excellently tailored dresses –
the furs whisked away at the door.
Cigarette smoke in the air.

Hitler and Himmler were the hosts.
The honor of being there!

Had it not been for Himmler's query:
"Do you have children?"
"We have a son."
He chided in the verbiage of the day:
"Germany needs sons!
You must bear more sons."

Erich and Hildegard Petschauer's second son, Klaus
Petschauer, when he was a year old. Photograph was
taken, most likely, by Erich Petschauer. Original
photograph is in author's inventory.

The young woman stood as if made of stone –
she thought she said:
"We cannot order sons.
That is not in our hands."

Did my mother realize already then
the extent of this man's arsenal of evil?
Or was she inspired by his words?
Nine months later,
she bore her second son in San Remo,
far away from Bavaria!

Munich's *Bayerischer Hof.*
Five stars then –
five stars now.
Odd conversations
in the ballroom 80 years ago,
on the terrace today.

*I presented this poem at the International Psychohistorical Association meeting, New York University, June 4th, 2016. My wife Joni and I visited the *Bayrischer Hof* when I had discovered that Heinrich Himmler, the chief of the SS, approached my mother during a party of SS and other NS political leaders in 1940. Joni and I drank coffee on the veranda, thinking and talking about that unique exchange.

From CBS News article, July 1st, 2013:
https://www.cbsnews.com/pictures/the-battle-of-gettysburg-150-years-later/

THE BATTLEFIELD*
(2018-2020)
For the families who lost one or more of their own on a front

A crumbling fence of wood and wires,
an overgrown stump,
a barely discernable crater.

Here they stumbled and fell,
soldiers of another time –
taking with them ambitions of their generals.

Most generals died in their beds,
now rest in the family crypt.
Soldiers succumbed in the field,
covered by the earth drenched with their blood.

*The battle of Gettysburg, at the outset of July 1863, was on my mind
when I wrote this poem.

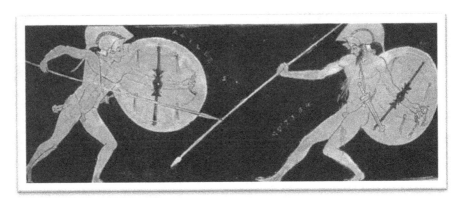

The Ancient vase-rendering of the ultimate battle between Achilles and Hector gives us a classic interpretation of Achilles on the attack, and Hector on the defensive and injured. One wound is visible on his left thigh, another below his right knee, and still another, more serious, below the right nipple. Achilles appears eager, head raised with open eyes and coming in for the final thrust; Hector stumbles backward with his head lowered and his spear attempting to parry his attacker's spear.

ANCIENT KILLERS – MODERN IMITATORS
(SPRING 2022)
*In Memory of Madeleine Albright**

I admired their strength, intelligence, swiftness, and bravado –
their godlike skill to surmount any obstacle.
Achilles, Odysseus, Hector, Alexander, Caesar –
my childhood heroes.
I conquered Troy with Achilles and Odysseus –
admired the battle-hardened strength of one
and the life-saving shrewdness of the other.

I defended Troy against the all-powerful Greek fleet.
With Priam and Hecuba,
I watched from its mighty walls as Thesis' son
dragged Hector's body in the dirt behind his chariot.
Soon after I cried over the death of this victor as well.

For ten years I wandered with his friend
about the Mediterranean Sea –
admired Penelope's loyalty as she wove at her carpet,
and hailed Odysseus as he slaughtered her suitors upon his return.

I rode with the Macedonian king as far as India –
fought in every battle along the way.
The date of every one of them imprinted in my mind to this day –
333 bei Issus Keilerei
331 Alexander gab dem Perser eins.

I replayed the Ides of March when treacherous senators,
led by Caesar's adopted son killed this warrior genius.
With his troops I had built bridges
over rushing rivers in faraway Gallia.
I stepped with him over the Rubicon.
Kai sy, teknon!
You too, my child!
All this forever chiseled in my head.

Heroes, yes, but also
arrogant, haughty, self-absorbed, and ruthless –
barely a thought of those whom
they killed, wounded, or ran off into slavery.

Boys and old men killed like cattle,
women pushed into slavery,
mere "objects" to marry off, if they were so "lucky."
Waiting for the men to return as heroes in triumph
or on their shields –
that was the fate of Spartans' loyal wives.

Despots really,
abusers, torturers, rapists, murderers –
ruthless destroyers of farms, cities, and civilizations.
Death and destruction wherever they went.

Why not see that other side?
Why not discuss it in Greek and Latin classes?
Why, in Catholic monasteries, remain unaware of these calamities?
Why not discern relationships between violence then
and European autocrats' horrific abuses later?

This is why!
We disdained conquers from the East –
Attila, Alaric, Genghis Khan, Tamerlane and all the rest.
These "others" –
vicious outliers, leaders of "barbarian hordes."
We ignored the same ruthless behavior
in our idols,
gloried instead in the newcomers' gore.

When time came to support,
or to explain to ourselves,
men like Hitler and others of his ilk,
we looked eastward once again –
we saw Stalin then,
we see Orban, Erdogan, and Putin now.
We abhor these tyrants' dastardly deeds.

Deep in our psyche,
we pushed aside the evil in our midst.
Our Ancient heroes,
we read,
reformed and uplifted civilizations:
Persia turned Greek and Gallia Roman.

TROUBLES

We saw reforms in our time as well:
The swamps drained near Rome
and *Volkswagen* and *Autobahnen* built in tandem.

Ignoring "our" Ancient heroes' violence
lured us to overlook to our detriment,
that of potentates in our midst.

They sell shiny reforms
as they grab power –
then hang on to it until the end.
Their aim is to undermine our liberties,
to inflate their freedoms to act at will.
This, while the planet is tortured to death
before our very eyes.

Let me cry with Cassandra
over the death of Hector, her brother,
defender of Troy and its freedoms,
however illusory they may appear.

The fickle gods,
created in the image of Ancient men and women,
punished evil men like Achilles and Pyrrhos Neoptolemos, his son.
But like our callous leaders,
they did not concern themselves with "lesser" human beings –
they were left to fend for themselves then,
just as we are now.

*Madeleine Albright was a fellow immigrant, served as US
representee to the UN and Secretary of State under President Bill
Clinton. She wrote the insightful analysis of authoritarianism,
Fascism. A Warning (New York, 2018). She died in 2022.

Richard Hildebrandt (left, standing) and Ulrich Greifelt (right) at the RuSHA trial in Nuremberg in March of 1948. Both were given life sentences. Greifelt died in captivity and Hildebrand was transferred to Poland, where he was retried and shot.*

Ready details about Hildebrandt are available at https://nl.wikipedia.org/wiki/Richard_Hildebrandt; details about Greifelt are at https://en.wikipedia.org/wiki/Ulrich_Greifelt.

THE SEARCH FOR MEANING
(2019-2020)

I looked for meaning and failed with every attempt.
I searched for understanding,
but those who came forward were of a different time and place.
I found love and it comforted me.

Foolishly I looked again.
In search for meaning!
You, who caused the anguish.
You said you made a mistake –
when you were young,
a long time ago.
You said the party bosses were tricksters,
only interested in their own success.
You fell for the lie.
They were not patriots,
just abusers of others' hopes and dreams.

Some call it intergenerational trauma.
Whatever the label –
it is the searing condition that hampers the wish to be oneself.

We can't choose our fathers.
We can't choose our mothers.
Their sins are not our sins,
and their mistakes are not ours.

Yet their decisions sit on us like rocks in a field,
or molecular scars on our DNA.
They weigh us down with searches
no child should ever have to undertake.

Your bosses have become our bosses –
mercilessly pursuing their nefarious goals.
Let me remind us:
If we are not in charge ourselves others are.

*My father was usually known as Dr. Erich Petschauer; he died in the fall of 1977 at almost 70 years of age. Greifelt and Hildebrandt were upper-level SS officers and Erich Petschauer's overall supervisors in Brixen/Bressanone and Berlin. Petschauer was stationed as the local administrator from 1939 until September 1943 in Brixen to persuade South Tyroleans, Austrian-German speaking Italian citizens, to leave Italy and return "Home to the Reich." From then until April 1944, he worked in Berlin as a liaison between his office and the national office of the NSDAP, the Nazi party. After being dismissed from that office over differences with Greifelt, he was in Bad Ischl and from April until May 8, 1945, at the front. He was captured by American forces on that day in a field of Upper Austria with about 300,000 other soldiers and officers.

Other supervisors in Italy were Werner Lorenz, his immediate chief in South Tyrol early on, and Otto Hofmann, another supervisor, responsible as well for the Italian activities. They too were tried in Nuremberg in the RuSHA process.

I discussed my father's role as an NS functionary, and these men and their relationships to him, in detail in Peter W. Petschauer, *Der Vater und die SS. Erich Petschauer und das NS-Regime* (Weger Buchhandlung, 2007), pp. 151ff.

Even though the Wikipedia articles are more detailed and in English, the best ready overall collection of these perpetrators is in Ernst Klee, *Das Personenlexikon zum Dritten Reich. Wer war was vor und nach 1945* (Fischer Taschenbuch Verlag, 2005).

MORE ABOUT THE AUTHOR

Joni Petschauer, author's wife, and the author – in the Spaten in Munich on April 18th, 2022. Photograph is by the author's grandniece Sabine Jahns; used here with her permission. Photograph is in the author's inventory.

Peter W. Petschauer, Ph.D., Dr. h. c., is Professor Emeritus of History of Appalachian State University, as well as a Research Associate of the Psychohistory Forum and a member of the editorial boards of *Clio Psyche* and *The Journal of Psychohistory*. He is also a member of the Scientific Advisory Board of German Association for Psychohistory and Political Psychology (GPPP).

After obtaining a Ph.D. in European and Russian History at New York University, Petschauer taught European history at Appalachian State University from 1968 to 2006. Aside from having held a named professorship, he led several programs, including Russian and East European Studies, the Hubbard Center for Faculty and Staff Support, as well as headed Appalachian's Faculty Senate and the University of NC System's Faculty Assembly. In May 2014, Appalachian granted him the Dr. h. c. in the Arts and Humanities.

Since the couple's retirement from the university, they concentrated on visits to family in South Tyrol, lower Austria, and Germany, especially to their granddaughter in Baden-Württemberg. The most joyful activity remains visiting museums here and abroad and continuing with their own collecting. They both are additionally engaged with Appalachian's Turchin Center for Visual Art and the An Appalachian Summer Festival.

In his research, the author has recently concentrated on a book of poems (published in NY, 2019) and his adjustment to the US in the 1960s (published in Charleston, 2020). His most recent research interests include book about what he learned in elementary school in Afers, "his" village in the Dolomites (published in Brixen/Bressanone, 2022), and a second poetry book (in print, NY, 2022). Other interests include the history of childhood, authoritarianism, and inter- and transgenerational trauma.

Dr. Petschauer may be contacted at petschauerpw@appstate.edu or peterpetschauer.com.

ENDORSEMENTS OF THIS VOLUME

66 "I searched for understanding." This is a line in one of the last poems found in *Listen to Rarely Heard Voices* and it reflects a thread that flows throughout. Petschauer may not yet have found understanding, but it is certain this text helps us all to consider understanding in new ways. Peter Petschauer's newest book of poetry carries us into his life as "acorns crash" and tyrants spread misery with "unmeasured glee." His figurative language shifts us between the sublime and the uncanny and gifts us with his links to nature, family and friends, and meanings of life. As the poems draw you deeper into the book, Petschauer graces us with fragments of his remarkable life. With his willingness to share his most intimate emotions, his poetry reflects angst, trauma, and joy in ways that encourages readers to reflect on their own life, to strive for understanding. *Listen to Rarely Heard Voices* by Peter Petschauer is a must read, the delightful and painful musings of a man greatly invested in all of humanity.

Amy C. Hudnall, M.A., is the Senior Lecturer at the Departments of History and Cultural, Global, and Gender Studies; Advisory Board and Faculty member, Center for Judaic, Holocaust, and Peace Studies; Fellow, Human Dignity and Humiliation Studies.

66 There is an enveloping presence to Peter Petschauer's poems in *Listen to Rarely Heard Voices*, like a cocoon inviting the reader to live inside them for a while. What a gift to experience, alongside the author, the warm moments of intimacy balanced with vast, sometimes jarring vistas reflecting the majesty of nature. I found myself dreaming these juxtapositions, wondering where – to use Petschauer's own evocative words from the book's opening – "we made the turn that took us." So much turn-taking comprises this book: at being young and old, good and evil, hidden and found. The rarely heard voices that speak through these oscillations are, at times, deeply familiar, at other times, strange and distant. All the while the call is to *listen* – not just see, but feel the wounds, and the joys, of a life lived fully, generously, and honestly as oneself. It is as if Petschauer is saying (but really showing) to us that it's possible to forget how to remember, and remember how to forget, and yet still live in a space of presence, without memory and desire.

Nathan Gerard, Ph.D., is the Associate Professor at California State University, Long Beach, in the Department of Health Care Administration, and Research Associate of the Center for Psychosocial Organization Studies.

❝ Peter Petschauer's arresting new volume of poems, *Listen to Rarely Heard Voices*, is a stunning commemoration of greed, avarice, power-gone-mad and the blood that drenches history, up to this very moment, at its behest. Indeed, the cautionary advice in each of these wonderfully narrative poems is to never forget the infamy history has habitually wrought, to remain ever-vigilant: "If we are not in charge ourselves – others are." Petschauer is a documentary poet of great cinematic range, a poet of witness. Nothing escapes his gaze; he invests in the abiding thunder of the image.

Joseph Bathanti, M.A., is the inaugural McFarlane Family Distinguished Professor in Interdisciplinary Education at Appalachian State University, North Carolina Poet Laureate and recipient of the 2016 North Carolina Award in Literature. His recent book is *Light at the Seam* (Louisiana State University Press, 2022).

❝ The subject of Peter Petschauer's latest book of poetry, *Listen to Rarely Heard Voices,* is that confluence point of noticing, attention, knowing, refusal *not to know* what one knows, and keen observation of the tiniest detail in the natural world to the largest canvas of history and culture. Petschauer brings these virtues to every topic he touches and to each poem he writes: Nature, family life and history, and the immense scale of history of societies – from ancient Western civilizations to Nazi Germany, to the Age of Trump and coronavirus. Often, as in the life of his father as an SS officer, family and society and the poet's personal development fatefully meet. Free of poetic conceit, Petschauer's style as poet is direct, concise, and clear.

The poems of Petschauer's book give great breadth and depth to what is perhaps the pivotal word in his title: *Listen*. The polyphony of voices who speak in his poems are voices we so often *wish not to hear* and *cannot bear to hear, let alone heed*. To truly listen is to bear witness; it is to affirm that "This Is." If we humans and our endangered planet are to survive, we must listen to these voices. With British soldier-poet Wilfred Owen, who was killed in World War I, Petschauer says in different words, "All a poet can do today is warn." That is the message, gift, and weight of this book.

Howard Stein, Ph.D., Professor Emeritus, Department of Family and Preventive Medicine, University of Oklahoma Health Sciences Center, Oklahoma City, OK. Author of ten books and scrapbooks of poetry, about 22 clinical and scholarly books, and hundreds of articles and chapters of books.

ENDORSEMENTS OF THIS VOLUME

❝ Peter Petschauer's *Listen to Rarely Heard Voices* is a joy to read. His poems range from beautiful observations of nature to glimpses of the ugliest deeds and thoughts humanity can harbor. All are little masterpieces of literature, filled with unexpected turns of light and dark. There is no artifice of sentimentality in them, just insight, illumination, and surprise.

Zohara Boyd, Ph.D., Professor Emeritus of English, Appalachian State University, Boone, NC. Dr. Boyd, along with her father, his wife, and his younger sister survived in plain sight in Warsaw during WWII.

❝ Peter W. Petschauer's *Listen to Rarely Heard Voices* has such beauty and richness that it touches me deeply at various levels – as it should many readers. It is a product of the life experience of a very special human being who may be a fairly new poet, but whose poetry is enriched by his incredible knowledge, sensibility, and wisdom. His poems carry the burden and beauty of the last eighty years we humans have shared. I hope you will read it.

Paul H. Elovitz, Ph.D., is a Historian, Research Psychoanalyst, Professor at Ramapo College, director of the Psychohistory Forum, and editor, *Clio's Psyche*. He is author of *The Making of Psychohistory: Origins, Controversies, and Pioneering Contributors* and hundreds of other publications.

CPSIA information can be obtained
at www.ICGtesting.com
Printed in the USA
LVHW060239090723
751827LV00004B/261

9 781942 431206